Greek Legends

THE STORIES • THE EVIDENCE

Written and illustrated by
PETER CONNOLLY

MACDONALD YOUNG BOOKS

CONTENTS

1. THE GORGON'S HEAD

THE GIRL FROM THE SEA

A young fisherman stood on the sea-shore, one stormy day, watching a large chest bobbing up and down in the surf. He cast his net over it, and pulled it towards him. It was heavier than he expected. He lifted the lid. Inside he found a girl of about fourteen, and a baby.

They were still alive, so the young fisherman took them both in his arms, and carried them up to his brother's palace, where their wet clothes were removed and replaced with warm blankets. The baby soon recovered, but it was many hours before the girl stirred. Suddenly her hand reached out.

"Where is my baby?" she cried.

"He is fine," the fisherman assured her. "Let me introduce myself. I am Dictys, brother to the king of Seriphos. But tell me, who are you, and who put you in that chest?"

"I am Danaë," said the girl. "And my father is king of Argos. One day the oracle told him that he would never have a son, but that I would bear him a grandson – a grandson who would kill him. After that he forbade me to marry, and imprisoned me in a dungeon. Zeus, the father of the gods, visited me there, disguised as a shower of gold dust, and after his visit my son, Perseus, was born. My father learned about my baby, of course, but he could not bring himself to kill us. So he put us in a chest and threw us into the sea."

Dictys put his arm round her.

"I will look after you both," he promised. "No one will find you here on this island."

Dictys cast his net out over the waves and snared the chest. He hauled it up on to the rocks. It was far heavier than he expected.

PERSEUS MAKES A PLEDGE

Dictys raised Perseus as his own son. The years passed, and Perseus grew into a handsome young man. But a cloud hung over them all. Dictys' elder brother, King Polydectes, wanted to marry Danaë, but Danaë hated him and continually rejected his advances. When the king persisted, Perseus warned him to leave his mother alone.

The king devised a clever plan to get rid of Perseus. He announced that he was planning to marry the beautiful Hippodameia instead.

"But I am poor," said the King. "I cannot afford to give her father a gift large enough to win her. I need every nobleman to give me something towards her dowry."

Perseus fell silent as the noblemen pledged their gifts.

"And what will you pledge, Perseus?" asked the king.

"You know I have nothing," Perseus replied. "But I will do anything you wish, if you will leave my mother alone."

"You will do anything to protect her, won't you," sneered the king. "You would even fight a Gorgon."

"Yes, I would fight a Gorgon, and bring you its monstrous head," replied Perseus.

"I accept," cried the king. "And my noblemen are witnesses to your pledge."

Perseus knew he had been tricked into a promise he could not keep. His mother would be unprotected, and he himself would face certain death, for the Gorgons were three terrible monsters, half woman, half beast, with snakes for hair and tusks like wild boars. Anyone who looked on them would be turned to stone.

ONE EYE, ONE TOOTH

That night Perseus was visited by the goddess Athena and the god Hermes. They took him to the island of Samos, where they asked him to study three statues of the Gorgons.

"You must be able to recognise Medusa," said Athena. "Only she is mortal. If you attack her sisters, you will die."

She gave him a polished shield and a crystal sword, one to protect him from Medusa's gaze, and the other for cutting off her head.

"You will also need Hades' helmet to make you invisible, a pair of winged boots, and a silver satchel in which to put Medusa's head," said Athena. "The Stygian Nymphs have these, but only the Old Women can tell you where to find the nymphs."

The Old Women were sisters of the Gorgons. They had only one eye and one tooth between the three of them, and they kept watch, warning the Gorgons if anyone approached.

Perseus found them living in semi-darkness in a deep valley at the foot of the Atlas mountains. As he hid behind a rock, he saw the hag on guard pass the eye and the tooth to one of her sisters. "It's your turn now, Enyo," she said.

Perseus crept forward silently until he was behind the sisters, and awaited his opportunity. When it was time for the third sister to stand guard, Perseus was ready for her. He snatched the eye before she could take it.

The third sister groped for the eye. "Where is it? Have you dropped it?" she asked Enyo.

"If you want it back, you must tell me where to find the Stygian Nymphs," said Perseus.

The hags were helpless without their eye, so they reluctantly told him what he wanted to know.

As the third sister groped for the eye, Perseus darted in. This was the chance he had been waiting for. Now they would have to tell him what he wanted to know.

10

THE FACE OF DEATH

The Stygian Nymphs were eager to help Perseus, and they willingly gave him the sandals, the helmet and the satchel. He put on the helmet of invisibility, and flew on up the valley past the three hags still guarding the pass towards the Gorgon's den. He could see reflected in his polished shield some grotesque figures. Perseus was puzzled for a moment, but then he realised that these were the frozen bodies of those whom the Gorgons had turned to stone. And there, amongst them, were the three hideous sisters.

Perseus recognised Medusa at once. He tried to approach her from behind, but she sensed his presence, and looked round. Perseus saw her face reflected in the shield, her fangs gnashing, as her eyes searched for him. Her mouth opened, and she hissed like a wildcat. Perseus tried to move in close several times, but she lashed out at him. He would never get close enough to kill her. Utterly dejected, he withdrew.

"Don't despair, Perseus," said Athena. "When Medusa is asleep I'll fetch you."

That evening Athena led Perseus back to the Gorgon's den. He kept his eyes glued to the shield as they approached, and the snakes began to hiss. Medusa stirred and raised her head as Perseus swung the crystal sword with all his strength, cutting into her neck. The Gorgon gave one blood-curdling shriek and her head fell to the ground.

The other two Gorgons were now awake. Perseus grabbed Medusa's head and thrust it into the silver satchel. He slung it over his shoulder and flew off towards the mountain-tops, with the two Gorgons in pursuit, for though he was invisible, they could smell him. They chased him up the valleys and over the mountains, but finally Perseus managed to escape southwards into the desert.

Perseus tried to approach Medusa from behind, but she sensed his presence.

ANDROMEDA

Perseus set out for home along the north coast of Africa. Turning northwards from Egypt, he noticed a crowd gathered on a beach, watching a beautiful girl who was chained to a rock overhanging the sea. "What are you doing to that young girl?" he asked angrily. "Release her at once!"

"But she must be sacrificed, or the monster will kill us all," they told him.

Cassiopeia, the girl's mother, came forward. "It's my fault," she sobbed. "I said I was more beautiful than the goddesses, and Poseidon, the sea god, has punished me by sending a monster to destroy us, unless I sacrifice my daughter, Andromeda."

"I will kill the monster," cried Perseus, "if, in return, I may marry Andromeda."

Cassiopeia agreed to this, and putting on his helmet of invisibility, Perseus flew low over the waves. But the monster saw his shadow reflected in the water, and snapped at it. Perseus swerved upwards, and then dived, driving his sword into the monster's back. The beast writhed in agony, its tail lashed the water, then it disappeared beneath the sea.

The crowd cheered – but they fell silent when the monster reappeared, rearing high above Perseus. The young hero darted clear of the monster's gnashing teeth; stabbing at its soft belly. It

Perseus donned his helmet of invisibility to rescue Andromeda.

lunged, knocking him into the water. Perseus struggled to a rock and reached into the silver satchel for Medusa's head. Before he could draw it out, the monster vanished beneath the waves for ever . . .

Perseus released Andromeda and led her back to her mother, claiming her hand in marriage as his reward. But now the monster was dead, Cassiopeia had second thoughts about her daughter marrying a stranger. So though she prepared for the wedding, she secretly sent for Andromeda's former suitor.

The guests were seated at the wedding feast, when suddenly Andromeda's jilted lover burst in with two hundred armed men. He hurled his spear at Perseus, but the young hero grabbed it and threw it back, killing an attacker. He then drew Hermes' sword and charged, but though he fought like a lion, the assailants kept coming.

"Kill him!" Cassiopeia screamed.

Perseus shouted to Andromeda to cover her eyes. Then he drew out Medusa's head and held it up. Everyone gasped, and suddenly there was silence, for they were all turned to stone. Cassiopeia's beauty was frozen for ever.

Perseus took Andromeda in his arms and flew back home with her to the island of Seriphos.

15

THE RETURN OF THE HERO

Perseus found Polydectes at the palace, banqueting with his friends, and strode into the centre of the room to confront the king.

"I have brought you what I promised," he said.

The king and his guests laughed mockingly. Then Polydectes held up his hands for silence, and said with a sneer: "Let us see what you have brought."

Perseus reached into the silver satchel, turning his eyes away, and Polydectes' mocking smile froze on his face as he looked on the Gorgon's head.

The guests were all turned to stone as they looked on Medusa's head.

THE PROPHECY FULFILLED

Danaë returned to Argos with Perseus and Andromeda. They found the palace deserted, for the old king had fled for fear of his grandson killing him.

Some months later they were invited to attend the funeral games of the king of Larissa. In the discus competition Perseus made a magnificent throw, but the discus, caught by the wind, flew into the crowd, hitting an old man. Danaë and Perseus rushed to the spot, but the old man was already dead. Danaë knew without looking that it was her father. The prophecy had been fulfilled.

Perseus felt unable to inherit the throne in such circumstances, and so he divided the kingdom with his cousin, ruling his half from the citadel at Tiryns. Many years later he reunited the kingdom and moved to Mycenae, which was to become the most famous citadel in Greece.

Perseus and Andromeda supervise the building of their new citadel at Mycenae. The later Greeks were so impressed by the massive stones used that they believed it was built by the Cyclopes, a race of one-eyed giants.

17

2. THE GREAT HERO

THE BIRTH OF A STRONG MAN

On Perseus' death his son, Electryon, became king, but was accidentally killed by his daughter Alcmene's husband, Amphitryon. Electryon's brother, Sthenelus, seized the throne and banished them both in disgrace.

They fled to Thebes, where Alcmene gave birth to twin boys. One was fathered by her husband, but the other, Hercules, or Heracles, by Zeus, king of the gods. This child was to become the most famous of all Greek heroes.

Zeus' wife, Hera, hated her husband's illegitimate child and sent two huge snakes to kill him. Though he was only a few months old, Hercules strangled them both with his bare hands, for Zeus had given him superhuman strength. But he had also cursed Hercules with a violent and explosive temper.

The city of Thebes had given shelter to Hercules and his mother, and he looked upon it as his home. When he was eighteen, he learned that it had been defeated by Orchomenos and forced to pay tribute to the king. Hercules returned to the city in fury, mutilating and throwing out the tribute collectors. He then led the young men of Thebes against Orchomenos, and killed the king.

The king of Thebes was so grateful to the hero that he gave him Megara, his daughter, as his bride.

Thebes enjoyed peace for a few years, but the Euboeans, old allies of Orchomenos, were determined to seek revenge. Hercules led the Thebans against them, routed their army, and captured the king. He showed no mercy. The king was tied hand and foot to two horses, who tore him apart.

Hercules' savagery horrified even the gods – but worse was to come. Hera still hated Hercules, and in spite, she brought down a fit of madness upon him. He attacked his own children, and threw their bodies on to a fire. Then, racked with guilt, he shut himself away, but found no peace of mind. He went to the oracle at Delphi, and sought advice from the priestess there. She ordered him to go to Tiryns, to become the servant of Eurystheus for twelve years.

"He will set you ten labours, and when you have completed them, you will become immortal," she said.

CORFU

Eli

Hercules was the great strong man of Greece. When less than a year old he strangled two huge snakes with his bare hands.

18

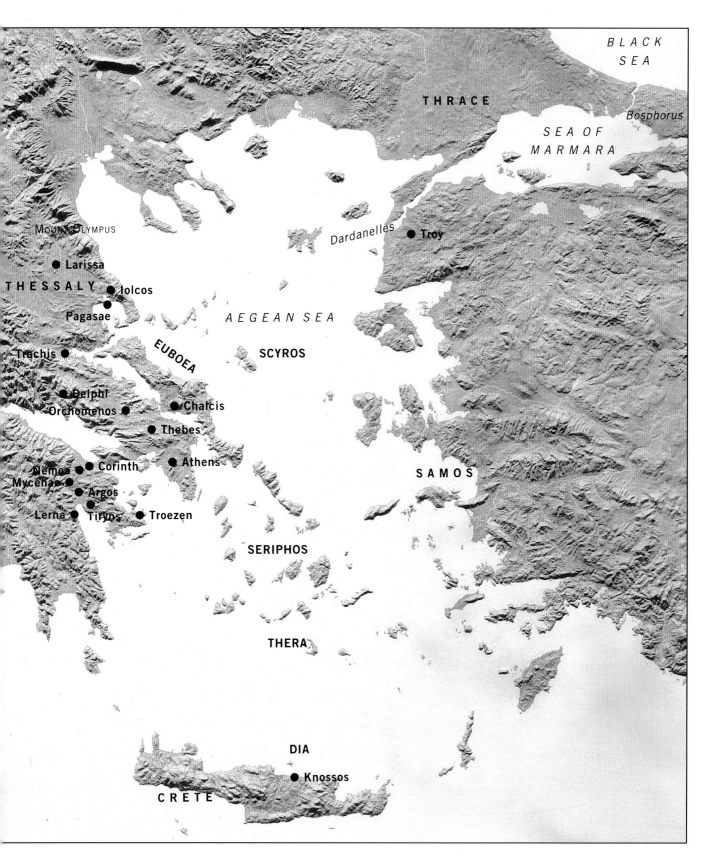

BLACK
SEA

THRACE

Bosphorus

SEA OF
MARMARA

Dardanelles ● Troy

MOUNT OLYMPUS

● Larissa

THESSALY ● Iolcos

Pagasae ●

AEGEAN SEA

Trachis ●

EUBOEA SCYROS

● Delphi

Orchomenos ● ● Chalcis

● Thebes

● Athens

Nemea ● ● Corinth

Mycenae ●

● Argos SAMOS

Lerna ● ● Tiryns ● Troezen

SERIPHOS

THERA

DIA

● Knossos

CRETE

19

THE LION OF NEMEA

Eurystheus was the son of Sthenelus, who had banished Hercules' mother, and was now king of Mycenae. He was terrified of Hercules, ever fearing that he might seize the throne. Now knowing that the young man was entirely at his mercy, he decided to send him on the most dangerous missions he could devise. The first of these was to hunt down a massive man-eating lion that was ravaging the countryside around Nemea.

Hercules tracked the lion to its den, hid in the bushes, and awaited its return. When the huge beast appeared, its jaws still dripping with human blood, Hercules tried to shoot it, but the arrow bounced off the lion's hide. Drawing his sword, he charged in, thrusting at its heart, but the sword buckled. Hercules now realised that no weapon could pierce the lion's heart, so next he attacked it with his club. He whirled the great weapon round his head, and brought it crashing down on the lion's nose. The club shattered, but the lion merely shook its head as if bothered by a fly and withdrew to its lair.

The cave where the lion was hiding had two entrances. Hercules blocked one entrance and entered by the other. The lion wanted to sleep after its meal, and snarled at him, but Hercules closed in warily, moving from side to side, waiting for an opportunity to attack.

Suddenly he saw his chance, and leapt forward. The lion snapped at him, biting off one of his fingers. Wincing with pain, Hercules landed on the lion's back, grasping it round the neck with both arms. The lion rolled on the ground, lashing out with its claws and fighting desperately for breath, as Hercules squeezed tighter and tighter. The lion grew weaker with every gasp, until it finally went limp and Her-

The first labour Eurystheus imposed on Hercules was to track down and kill the gigantic lion of Nemea. The great hero wore the lion's skin as his armour for the rest of his life.

cules relaxed his grip. He staggered to his feet, rested for a few minutes, then heaved the huge carcass on to his shoulders and set out for Mycenae, where he threw it down at Eurystheus' feet.

The king's fear of Hercules now turned to abject terror. He withdrew to a metal underground chamber that he had had constructed outside the city walls and would only speak to Hercules through a herald.

Hercules skinned the lion, using one of its claws as a knife. He wrapped its pelt around his body, and wore its head as a helmet. This was to be his only armour.

21

KILL THE HYDRA

Hercules was soon called to Mycenae once again. Eurystheus hid in his chamber while his herald gave the orders. They were for Hercules to kill the Hydra.

The Hydra was said to be indestructible. It lived in a swamp at Lerna on the far side of the Gulf of Argos, and had nine snakelike heads. Its breath and even the scent of its footprints were so venomous that they could kill.

Hercules cut himself a new club from an olive tree, and set out for Lerna with his nephew, Iolaus. His task seemed impossible, but just as he was despairing the goddess Athena appeared. "Hera hates you so much that she reared this monster specially to kill you," she said. "But I will help you as I helped your great-grandfather, Perseus, kill Medusa. The Hydra has a weakness. It hates fire."

The goddess handed Hercules a golden sword. "Cut off its middle head with this, but bury it deep, for it is immortal."

Hercules attacked the monster with fire arrows, driving it into the shallows of the swamp. Then he waded out to meet it, with his lion's skin wrapped tightly round him. The nine heads hissed menacingly as he approached, the waters swirled and the creature's tail coiled round him, trying to drag him down. One of the Hydra's many heads darted towards him, and Hercules struck it with his club, crushing it to pulp. But to his horror two new heads grew in its place. Again he crushed them, but now three heads appeared.

Iolaus watched from the shore. He set the trees around the swamp alight, hoping to frighten the monster, then he grabbed a flaming branch, and waded out to help his uncle. As Hercules hit another head, Iolaus plunged the burning brand into the wound. The Hydra's blood bubbled, but no new heads grew.

Hera was watching the fight, and grew ever angrier as Hercules and Iolaus destroyed the monster's heads. She sent a giant crab to help the Hydra, but Hercules stamped on it with such force that he smashed its shell. Only one head now remained, and though Hercules struck it again and again, he could not crush it. Then, remembering Athena's words, he drew the golden sword and severed it with one clean blow. He buried the head, still hissing, on the edge of the swamp under a huge rock, then cut open the monster's body, and dipped his arrows in its blood, so that even a scratch from them would now be fatal.

Hercules waded out into the swamp and attacked the many-headed Hydra with his club. Each time he crushed a head, two or three more grew in its place.

THE CERYNEIAN HIND

Hercules' next task was more a test of stamina and skill than of bravery and strength. He was to catch alive the Ceryneian Hind. Though it was as large as a bull, it was swift and agile.

The great hero chased the deer over mountains and plains for a whole year, catching up with it at last as it was drinking at the river Ladon beyond the mountains to the west of Mycenae. He aimed carefully and pinned its front legs together, without drawing blood. Throwing the deer over his shoulder, he returned home. Eurystheus accepted the Hind grudgingly, then despatched Hercules over the mountains to catch an enormous wild and dangerous boar.

Above: *It took Hercules a year to complete his third labour – hunting down and capturing the Ceryneian Hind.*

THE DEATH OF CHEIRON

On his way to hunt the wild boar, Hercules visited his old friend, Pholus the centaur. Centaurs were half man and half horse, and generally they were violent and aggressive, though Pholus and the centaur's king, Cheiron, were both gentle and friendly.

Even the smell of wine can make centaurs drunk, so it was very reluctantly that Pholus opened a jar of wine when Hercules asked for it.

Soon the other centaurs smelt the wine. They burst into the cave, hurling rocks and logs. Hercules snatched two blazing timbers from the fire and fought them off, killing several, and driving the rest of them away.

The centaurs fled to their king, Cheiron, who was so renowned for his wisdom and knowledge of medicine that the gods had made him immortal. The fleeing centaurs crowded round him, and Hercules, following close behind, shot an arrow at one of them. It passed through the centaur's arm, but hit Cheiron on the knee.

The king clutched his leg in agony, and Hercules rushed forward to pull out the arrow. But it was too late – the Hydra's poison had already taken hold. Hercules treated the wound with Cheiron's own ointments, but nothing could relieve the pain.

Cheiron crawled back to his cave, writhing in agony and begging the gods to let him die. At last Zeus took pity on him, and did so.

Below: *While visiting his friend, Pholus the centaur, Hercules was attacked by a gang of drunken centaurs. The centaurs were generally savage and evil. Only Pholus and Cheiron were good.*

EURYSTHEUS TRIES TO HUMILIATE HERCULES

Saddened by the death of Cheiron, Hercules completed his task quickly. He chased the giant boar through the mountains, drove it into a snowdrift, and bound it with chains. Then he heaved it on to his shoulders and carried it back to Mycenae.

In the spring Eurystheus sent for Hercules again. The king had found a really degrading job for the hero. King Augeias of Elis had the largest and filthiest herds of cattle in the world. The gods had made the cattle immune from disease, so he never cleaned out their pens, and the stench was overwhelming.

Hercules realised Eurystheus' intention, but he controlled his temper, and set out for King Augeias' farm. The dung was so deep that he could not enter the yard, but he had a plan. He dug two trenches to

Hercules drove the Erymanthian Boar from its lair and then chased it across the mountains until it ran into a snowdrift.

Eurystheus found Hercules a really degrading job, but the hero outwitted him.

nearby rivers, and diverted them so that they flowed through the yard, washing everything clean. The king was so pleased by this that he gave Hercules some of his cattle as a reward.

THE DEADLY BIRDS

Hercules' next task was to destroy a huge flock of birds with bronze feathers, claws and beaks. They lived in the swamp at Stymphalus, and attacked people and animals by shooting at them with their bronze feathers.

Hercules was unable to get near the birds, for the swamp was covered with dense thickets, but once again Athena came to his aid. She gave him a bronze rattle, and the raucous din so terrified the birds that they soared into the air, screeching and shooting their deadly feathers everywhere. Hercules wrapped his lion skin tightly round him, and shot volley after volley of his poisonous arrows, killing many of the birds. The rest flew off to Ares' Island in the Black Sea.

The Stymphalian birds killed people by shooting at them with their bronze feathers.

YET MORE TASKS

Hercules was soon given his next task. Minos the king of Crete had promised to sacrifice anything that came out of the sea to the sea god Poseidon, but when a magnificent white bull emerged from the waves, he tried to substitute another bull for it. The gods punished him by making his queen fall in love with the bull.

The lovesick queen asked Daedalus the king's architect to build her a statue of a cow, so that she could get inside it and

Capturing the Cretan Bull was Hercules' seventh labour. Some say the bull swam back to Greece with Hercules on its back.

28

pretend to be the bull's mate. The result of her passion was the birth of a child, half man and half bull, called the Minotaur.

Hercules now hunted down the white bull that was terrorising the island, bringing it back to Mycenae, where Eurystheus dedicated it to Hera. But the goddess rejected it, because it had been caught by Hercules, and she released it. Once again it roamed the countryside, killing all who came near it.

Eurystheus now sent Hercules to Thrace, to bring back the carnivorous horses owned by the evil king Diomedes. Hercules and his men broke into the palace and drove the horses down to the

Hercules had left his young friend Abderus to guard the carnivorous horses, but they attacked the youth and ate him.

beach, pursued by the Thracians. Leaving his friend Abderus to guard the horses, Hercules ordered half his men to hold back the attackers and the other half to dig a channel from the sea to the plain. As the plain filled with water the Thracians retreated back to the palace.

But Hercules seized King Diomedes and dragged him to the horses. He found that Abderus had already been eaten. "Take him too," cried Hercules, and threw the king to his own terrible beasts. The horses now became docile, and Hercules drove them back to Greece. After this, he set off on an expedition to the Black Sea.

3. THE GOLDEN FLEECE

When their stepmother tried to kill them, Phrixus and Helle were saved by a golden ram which carried them off to the Black Sea. Helle fell from it as they crossed the Dardanelles, giving the strait its ancient name, the Hellespont.

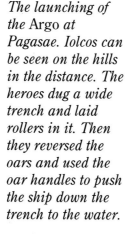

The launching of the Argo *at Pagasae. Iolcos can be seen on the hills in the distance. The heroes dug a wide trench and laid rollers in it. Then they reversed the oars and used the oar handles to push the ship down the trench to the water.*

BEWARE OF THE MAN WITH ONE SANDAL

Jason the Argonaut was smuggled out of the palace of Iolcos when his uncle Pelias seized the throne, and was brought up by Cheiron the centaur.

When he was a young man he returned to Iolcos to reclaim the throne. On the way he carried an old woman across a river, but lost one of his sandals midstream. He thought little of it, and travelled on to Iolcos.

Pelias turned pale when he saw Jason, for the oracle had warned him to beware of a man with one sandal.

"Who are you?" Pelias demanded. When Jason told him, he asked:

"What would you do if you met someone destined to kill you?"

"I would send him to bring back the Golden Fleece," said Jason. He had never heard of the Golden Fleece, but Hera, queen of the gods, had put the words into his mouth. It was Hera, too, who, disguised as the old woman, had made him lose his sandal and thus fulfil the prophecy.

"The palace is haunted by the ghost of Phrixus, son of King Athamas of Orchomenos," said Pelias. "He and his sister Helle were carried off by a golden ram, and Phrixus gave the ram's fleece to the king of Colchis. The oracle says that Iolcos won't prosper till the fleece is returned."

"I will endeavour to bring it back," Jason said to Pelias, "provided you give up the throne if I succeed."

Then he called for volunteers, and fifty heroes, including Hercules, all assembled on the beach at Pagasae where the ship, the *Argo*, was being built.

THE EXPEDITION SETS OUT

The crew, who became known as the Argonauts, sailed across the Aegean Sea and through the Dardanelles into the Sea of Marmara. Here the wind dropped and they had to row against the current. Very soon they were completely exhausted.

Hercules jeered and called them weaklings. For a little while, pride made them carry on, but one by one they dropped out until only Jason remained. He tried to keep pace with the great hero, but in the end his arms refused to move and he too gave up. Hercules then gave a great roar and pulled with all his strength, but his oar snapped, and he threw it angrily into the sea.

The heroes beached the ship at last, and Hercules set off to find a tree from which to make a new oar. On his return he discovered that his friend Hylas had disappeared, and so he searched all night for him, wandering far from the ship. At dawn a fresh breeze sprang up, and the Argonauts were keen to get under way. They shouted for Hercules, but he was too far away to hear. Finally they set sail without him.

The *Argo* sailed on eastwards towards the Bosphorus, the narrow channel leading to the Black Sea. Sailors ventured up it in constant fear of its treacherous currents.

Nearby lived the prophet Phineus who had offended the gods by foretelling the future too accurately. For this they made him old and blind. Not content with this, they sent two Harpies – creatures that were half-woman and half-bird – to fly down and poison Phineus' food with their droppings. The prophet was gradually starving to death.

The Argonauts begged Phineus to tell them if they would get safely past the Blue Rocks guarding the far end of the Bosphorus.

The Harpies soared into the air, pursued by Calais and Zetes, twin sons of the wind god, Boreas. They would have killed the Harpies if the gods had not intervened.

"I will tell you nothing unless you kill the Harpies," replied Phineus.

Two of the Argonauts, Calais and Zetes, were sons of the wind god and could fly. When the Harpies appeared, the two men pounced on them, and screeching with fear, the evil creatures flew up into the sky. The twins then pursued the Harpies, and would have killed them, but the gods intervened, promising to keep them away from Phineus. Now the old prophet told the heroes much of what they wanted to know.

"Take a dove, and when you reach the rocks, release it," he said. "If it flies through, follow it quickly. But turn back if it gets caught, or you will all die."

33

THE BLUE ROCKS

The Argonauts soon entered the narrow straits of the Bosphorus. The current hurled the *Argo* from side to side, threatening to smash it against the cliffs. Ahead of them they heard a sound like distant thunder, and as they rounded a bend in the channel they saw two mountainous blue rocks blocking it, drifting towards each other to collide with a thunderous crash.

The heroes released the dove, and it flew towards the gap between the rocks. They crashed together again, obscuring everything in spray. As it cleared, they saw the dove through the gap. It had made it.

"Row," shouted Jason and soon they were speeding towards the gap. The dove had flown free, but they had not noticed that its tail feathers were missing.

As the Argonauts entered the gap, the rocks began to close. "Pull," cried Jason. "Sweet Athena, help us, or we perish."

The rocks closed in fast, as a huge wave arched above them. They felt the bows rise, and rowed with all their strength. The *Argo* cut through the crest, its bows dropped, and they were riding down the back of the wave.

The *Argo* cleared the rocks, but they were driven back once again, and the rocks were now towering above them. Again Jason shouted to Athena, and braced himself for the crash.

Suddenly the ship jumped forward, and the rocks hesitated. Athena had come to their rescue. For a moment the *Argo* shuddered, held fast by her stern post. But the stern post broke, and they were through at last.

The Blue Rocks towered above the Argonauts.

34

THE PRIESTESS OF HECATE

The Argonauts rowed on for many days along the south coast of the Black Sea, passing the land of the Amazons. One night, after being attacked by the Stymphalian Birds which Hercules had driven out of Greece, they picked up four young men from a shipwreck. These were the sons of Phrixus, on their way to Greece to find their father's family. The Argonauts welcomed them and persuaded them to join the expedition.

Two days later the Argonauts saw the Caucasian Mountains rising above the horizon. Then the rugged coastline gave way to open fields, and they were in the land of the Colchians.

A mist over the coast hid their approach, and the sons of Phrixus guided them into the mouth of the river Phasis where they moored the *Argo*. Jason, accompanied by the sons of Phrixus, went up to the palace to see if King Aeëtes would surrender the Golden Fleece.

They slipped into the palace unnoticed. In the women's quarters they found Chalciope, mother of the sons of Phrixus, and her younger sister, Medea. Chalciope welcomed her sons, but Medea's eyes were drawn towards Jason. Her cheeks burned, and she blushed and turned away, her veil hiding her feelings.

Medea tried to look away, but her eyes were drawn irresistibly towards Jason. Eros' love arrow had pierced her heart.

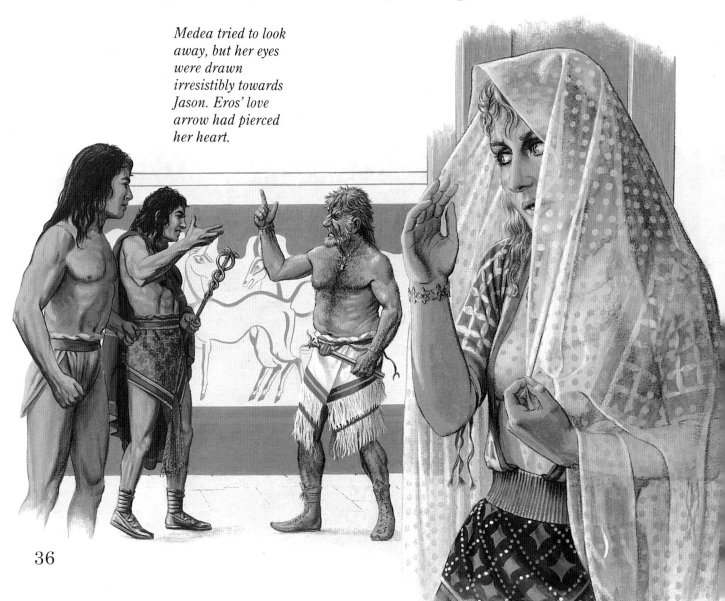

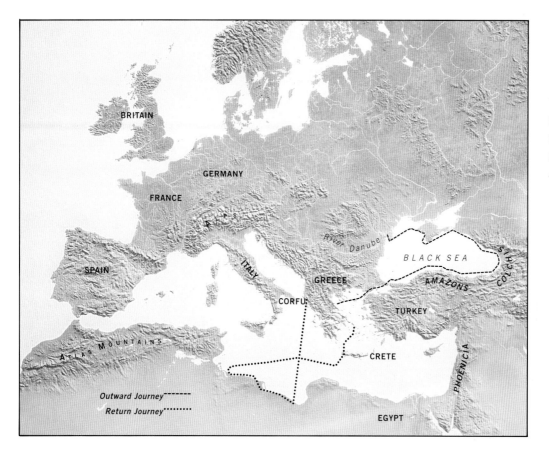

The Argonauts travelled far in their search for the Golden Fleece.

AEËTES SETS A TEST

Though the sons of Phrixus begged their grandfather to hand over the Golden Fleece, King Aeëtes could hardly contain his rage.

"Traitors!" he cried. "I know why you are here. You wish to kill me and seize my kingdom."

Jason explained to Aeëtes how he had been helped by Athena, and at this the king addressed him in a gentler tone.

"You may be telling the truth. I will arrange a test to see if the gods really are with you. It will require more than human power. I have two bulls with which I want you to plough the field of Ares. Then you must sow these – and reap whatever grows." He handed Jason a bag of dragon's teeth.

Jason had heard of Aeëtes' fire-breathing bulls with their bronze hoofs, and was horrified at the task before him. But he saw no way out; acceptance meant almost certain death, but Aeëtes would kill him anyway. He nodded his assent, and left the palace. Medea watched him go, and her heart went with him.

The Argonauts were horrified at the task before him, but one of Phrixus' sons offered a glimmer of hope.

"Our mother's sister, Medea, is a priestess of Hecate, the dark goddess. She is skilled in magic, and she might be able to help you."

That night the young Colchian returned to the palace to seek his mother's help, while in another room Medea lay awake, torn by her love for this young stranger, and the fear she had of her father. She cursed the gods, who had done this to her. Then she broke down and wept. Her maids fetched Chalciope, and Medea poured her heart out. Chalciope lifted Medea's tear-stained face, and told her how much Jason needed her help.

"Yes, I must help him," said Medea. "Send him a message to meet me alone at Hecate's shrine at daybreak."

37

AT THE SHRINE OF THE DARK GODDESS

Medea left the palace with her hand-maidens as dawn was breaking. When she reached the shrine she waited impatiently, constantly glancing along the path. Her heart leapt as she saw Jason striding towards her. Jason saw her lower her eyes, and spoke gently to her: "Don't be afraid. I won't harm you."

Medea did not raise her eyes, for fear of betraying her feelings. She handed him a small phial, and at that moment Jason saw her face. His heart missed a beat, he looked away and Medea found the courage to meet his eyes.

"You must come here at midnight," she said. "Bathe in the stream, and dress in grey. Dig a circular pit, and pile firewood around it. Sacrifice a ewe, burn it over the

Medea saw Jason striding towards her. The gods had cruelly made her fall in love with him. This began a tragedy that was to lead to many deaths. But now her handmaidens withdrew, leaving her alone with him.

38

pit, pour honey over it and pray to Hecate for help. Don't miss any part of this ritual, or all will be lost.

"At dawn tomorrow," she continued, "mix the charm I gave you with water and rub it into your body, and on your armour and weapons. It will make you invincible. When the dragon's teeth sprout from the furrows, throw a large stone amongst them." When she had told him all this, she turned to go.

"Remember me when you return to Greece," she said sadly and hurried away, her eyes downcast, for she dared not look at him again. But Jason called after her. "Sweet Medea, wait a moment. Will you come back to Iolcos with me, to be my bride?"

Medea was unable to speak. She knew her father would kill her rather than allow her to marry Jason. Her handmaidens led her, weeping, back to the palace.

THE HARVEST OF DEATH

Jason completed all the rituals, as Medea had told him. Then, accompanied by the Argonauts, he made his way to the field of Ares.

The Colchians screamed with delight as the bulls emerged from their underground pens. They expected to see Jason run, and his mangled body trampled underfoot. But Jason stood firm and braced himself for the onslaught.

The bulls crashed into his shield, and backed off, stunned. They charged again, breathing fire. The Argonauts gasped as they saw Jason disappearing in the smoke, but he emerged, unscathed. The bulls now tried to trample him with their bronze hoofs, but they were powerless against Medea's magic. They drew back, pawing the ground.

Jason seized one bull by the horns, kicked its front feet, and brought it to its knees. The second bull charged, but Jason dodged to one side, then knocked it to the ground, too.

He dragged them together, and tied the yoke across their shoulders. Then he urged them to their feet, and drove them forward, using his sword as a goad. They roared with pain, scorching the ground with their breath, as they ploughed the furrows and Jason planted the dragon's teeth.

The earth began to heave, and giants, armed with double-pointed swords, rose from the furrows. Jason shook with fear, but he remembered Medea's instructions, and hurled a huge boulder at them.

The bulls charged again and again, their fiery breath scorching the earth, but they were powerless against Medea's magic.

Jason charged into the battle, thrusting to the left and right. But more and more giants rose from the furrows.

"You threw that!" bellowed one of the giants, driving his sword into his companion. Soon each giant was killing his neighbour. Jason watched for a while, then plunged into the fight, thrusting to left and right with his sword. The crowd cheered, but Aeëtes guessed that Medea had betrayed him, and vowed vengeance on her and Jason.

The giants turned on Jason, but were unable to wound him. He killed them one by one, and then followed the furrows, killing the giants as they grew. When the slaughter was over, he walked confidently over to Aeëtes, demanding to be given the Golden Fleece.

"Never!" cried the king. "I will see you all dead first."

41

MEDEA

Medea did not sleep that night. She knew her father well, and had seen the look in his eyes. Her handmaidens would reveal her meeting with Jason under torture, and she knew he would not grant her a swift death. She remembered how he had treated others who had betrayed him.

She took out a bottle of poison, but as she was about to drink it the goddess Hera appeared. She rushed forward and dashed it from her hands.

"No, Medea, don't kill yourself," she said. "You must help Jason get the Golden Fleece, then you must leave with him."

Medea told her maids to prepare for the journey. She cut off a lock of her hair as a memento for her mother, then, with her casket of magic potions under her arm, she ran barefoot from the palace with her maids following.

Medea saw the glow of the Argonauts' campfire on the other side of the river. She called to them, and, recognising her voice, Jason ordered the heroes to row the *Argo* across. He jumped ashore before the boat touched the bank, and Medea threw herself at his feet.

"Save me from my father," she pleaded. "He knows that I helped you, and he will kill me. I will help you get the Golden Fleece, if you will take me away with you afterwards."

"Sweet lady, you know I love you," said Jason, "and may the gods bear witness to my oath. I promise to marry you, and to love you till the day I die."

Jason helped her aboard and the heroes rowed upstream until they came to the sacred grove. Medea and Jason jumped ashore and hurried up the path towards the shrine. They could see the Golden Fleece hanging on an oak tree, and glistening in the first rays of the sun.

The serpent guarding the fleece heard them coming. It opened its mouth and

hissed. The sound nearly shattered their eardrums, and echoed down the valley to the palace. Aeëtes sprang from his bed, shouting for his chariot.

Jason drew back at the sight of the monster, but Medea cut some sprigs of juniper, and advanced into the grove, singing softly. Jason followed, never taking his eyes off the serpent's head as it danced from side to side, the coils of its body writhing amongst the trees.

Jason was terrified when he saw the huge serpent guarding the Golden Fleece, but Medea advanced fearlessly, singing gently as she sprinkled her magic potion on the monster.

42

Medea took a bottle from her girdle, and dipped the juniper twigs in it. She moved closer, still singing, and sprinkled the serpent with the potion. As it gradually lowered its head, she brushed its eyelids with the twigs. Soon it was fast asleep.

As Jason darted forward, he could hear Aeëtes' men coming up the valley. He quickly climbed the tree, took the Golden Fleece, and slung it over his shoulder. Then they both ran for the ship.

Aeëtes' men had already arrived, but the Argonauts managed to hold back the attackers while Jason helped Medea aboard. They all rowed downstream under a hail of javelins, while Medea and her maids tended the wounded.

Aeëtes arrived in time to see the *Argo* disappear down the river. He vowed vengeance on Medea, and ordered his son, Apsyrtus, to launch the fleet and bring her back to him alive.

MURDER MOST FOUL

The Argonauts were terrified when they heard the voice of Zeus, king of the gods. He spoke to them through the figurehead of the Argo, *condemning Jason and Medea for their monstrous crime.*

Phineus, the blind prophet, had warned the Argonauts not to return the way they had come. So they headed north up the east coast of the Black Sea, past the Crimea, and on towards the mouth of the river Danube.

Meanwhile, the Colchians had sailed westwards. When they reached the Bosphorus, they learned from the local people that the Argonauts had not passed that way. So, leaving a guard, Apsyrtus sailed up the west coast, hoping to intercept the *Argo* there.

The Argonauts sailed into the northern outlet of the Danube delta. Apsyrtus guessed where they were, and he blocked the northern mouth. Then he sailed up the southern outlet until he reached the main river. The Argonauts could now go neither back to the sea nor up the river. They were trapped.

Outnumbered by ten to one, they looked round for someone to sacrifice to save their own skins. Their gaze settled on Medea.

"Aeëtes wants her, not us. Jason won the Fleece fair and square. They will let us go if we hand her over."

Medea looked at Jason.

"Will you do as they ask?" she demanded, but Jason did not reply.

"The cruel gods made me fall in love with you," she cried angrily. "I fought my emotions, but the gods drove me on. I betrayed my people for you. I lost my family and home, and now you, too, plan to hand me over to my father. What about your vow to the gods?"

Still Jason did not answer her.

Medea saw only one way out for them.

She must betray her own brother, for his men would be lost without a leader. She sent a message to Apsyrtus, claiming that she had been taken by force, and that she would help him get back the Golden Fleece, and then return with him to Colchis.

Jason agreed to this plan, and together they plotted her brother's death.

Apsyrtus agreed to meet Medea secretly at night on a small island, but when he arrived, Jason was lying in wait, and murdered him as he was greeting his sister. The rest of the Argonauts launched a surprise attack on Apsyrtus' ship, and killed the crew. Then they slipped past the Colchian vessels in the dark, and headed upstream.

The Argonauts had gone too far with Apsyrtus' murder, and the gods were angry. They lashed the *Argo* with storms day after day, driving them ever further from the world they knew.

One night the Argonauts heard Zeus himself thundering at Jason and Medea. "You will never reach Greece till you are cleansed of this foul murder," he said. "Only the witch Circe can save you."

The Argonauts rowed on for weeks. No one knew exactly where they went. But at last they reached the island of Aeaea where Circe ritually cleansed them of their guilt. They sailed on towards Greece, and finally reached the island of Corfu. There Jason married Medea as he had promised.

The Colchians, also on the island, tried to persuade the king of Corfu to hand over Medea. But the queen took pity on the couple, and begged her husband to let them go. The king then decreed that, since they were now married, Aeëtes no longer had any power over Medea.

TALOS, GUARDIAN OF CRETE

Medea came to the Argonauts' rescue once again, calling up demons from the underworld to drive Talos mad.

The Argonauts left Corfu, and sailed on. They caught sight of southern Greece, but Zeus was not yet satisfied that they had been punished enough. He sent a tempest, which drove the *Argo* southwards for nine days, till at last it was washed ashore on the North African coast. The waves carried the ship over sandbanks, forcing the Argonauts to drag it across the desert before they could relaunch it.

Parched with thirst, the Argonauts set sail for Greece once more, but their trials were not yet over. The wind dropped, and they had to row solidly for two days and two nights until they reached the island of Crete.

As they approached the shore a huge bronze figure hurled boulders at them from the clifftop. This was Talos, guardian of Crete, who could burn strangers to death by making himself red-hot. He had one single vein running from his head to his ankle.

Each time the Argonauts tried to land, Talos drove them back. Then Medea sang a hymn to Hecate, calling up demons to drive the giant mad.

Talos tried to hurl rocks at Medea, but under her spell his movements became clumsy, and he stumbled over a sharp pinnacle of rock, catching the end of his vein. His lifeblood flowed from him, and he fell to earth with a great crash.

The heroes beached the *Argo* and scrambled ashore, stopping only to take on fresh water. They then put to sea again and headed home, till at last they sailed into the Bay of Pagasae.

47

THE DEATH OF PELIAS

"What news from Iolcos?" Jason asked a fisherman, as the Argonauts rowed towards the beach. He learned from the man that the Argonauts were believed to be dead and that Pelias had killed Jason's parents.

Jason was devastated. There were too few of the Argonauts to storm the citadel successfully in order to kill Pelias, but once more Medea offered to help.

The heroes dragged the *Argo* up the beach, hiding it amongst the trees, while Medea made her preparations. She had a large wooden statue of the goddess Artemis, with a secret door in its base. Her handmaidens caught a young lamb which she put into a trance, and hid it inside the statue, together with the drugs that she needed. She rubbed potions into her skin until it became wrinkled and her hair entirely white. To all outward appearances, Medea was now an old woman.

The following day she set out in a chariot with the hollow statue beside her. She entered Iolcos, where she set up the statue in the square. It was not long before she was surrounded by a curious crowd. Medea spoke to them in a voice cracked with age.

"I have good news for you," she said. "Your king, Pelias, has found favour with the gods. They have promised to send prosperity to your town, and eternal youth to your king."

Medea sounded so convincing that everyone believed her. She was then called to the palace and repeated her story to the king and to his daughters. The old king's face betrayed his disbelief.

"I can give you proof that I have power over old age," said Medea, "if you do as I say." She turned to the princesses and asked that they should prepare a bath of pure water for her. She washed the magic potions from her skin, the wrinkles disappeared, and she became golden-haired and youthful again.

Pelias was so astonished at the transformation that he begged her to do the same for him. This was the moment the sorceress had been waiting for. Medea seated the old king on a couch and gazed intently into his eyes. Very soon Pelias had sunk into a deep trance. Then she asked the princesses to fetch a cauldron of boiling water.

"You must immerse him in it if he is to gain eternal youth," she said.

The girls looked horrified.

"You have no more faith in the power of the gods than your father," said Medea. "But I will show you what will happen. There is an old ram tethered outside the palace. Bring it to me."

When the ram was brought into the room, Medea sprinkled it with potions till it fell into a drugged sleep. She then cut it into thirteen parts and threw them in the boiling water. When she had done this she went to the wooden statue. As she bowed down to worship before it, she opened the secret door at the base, and when she rose to her feet again she held in her arms the young lamb she had hidden there.

"Now do you believe me?" she asked.

The princesses hesitated no longer. They seized their drugged father and cut him into pieces, which they threw into the cauldron while Medea chanted magic words. Then she smiled to herself. The deed was done, and yet she had never touched Pelias.

"Let us now take lighted torches up on the roof, to invoke the help of the moon goddess," she said.

The princesses followed Medea up on to the roof, waving their lighted torches to the moon. It was the signal for which Jason had been waiting. Finding the gates unguarded, the Argonauts stormed the town, and captured the citadel.

Pelias' daughters crowded round the cauldron of boiling water as Medea plunged in the old ram's head. Only one daughter, Alcestis, was suspicious, and refused to co-operate in her father's murder.

THE ARGONAUTS SPLIT UP

The great adventure was over. Jason and Medea should have lived happily ever after, but it did not happen that way. The people of Iolcos were outraged when they realised how Medea had tricked the princesses into murdering their father. The matter was brought before the council and the couple were banished.

So the *Argo* put to sea once more, and the heroes sailed south. They broke their journey to take the Golden Fleece to Orchomenos, Phrixus' birthplace, where they hung it in the temple of Zeus. Then they sailed on to Corinth, where they were greeted rapturously, for their fame had spread before them. They dragged the *Argo* ashore for the last time and the Argonauts split up.

THE FINAL TRAGEDY

Jason and Medea lived happily at Corinth for ten years and bore several children. Medea became famous for her wisdom and her ability to foretell the future. Aegeus, king of Athens, was one who sought her advice. She helped him interpret a strange saying from the oracle at Delphi, on condition that he gave her shelter should she ever need it.

This was no idle request, for Medea had foreseen that all was not well between Jason and herself. He had fallen in love with Glauce, daughter of the king of Corinth, and had already told Medea that he intended to divorce her in order to marry Glauce.

Medea was deeply shocked. "Do your vows to the gods mean nothing to you?" she cried, but Jason shouted back at her:

"You forced me to make them – I did not regard them as binding."

Glauce's dress ignited, engulfing her in flames. When her father tried to help he caught fire, too. Nothing would quench the flames. Soon the palace itself was ablaze.

"I gave up everything for you," sobbed Medea. "How many times have I saved your life? You would be nothing without me. And now you intend to desert me in a foreign land."

But Jason refused to listen.

Glauce loathed Jason's children, and considered them a threat. She was determined to get rid of them. She persuaded her father to banish Medea and the children, and when Medea refused to go, the king declared he would kill them all.

At this threat Medea appeared to accept the situation, and on the morning of the wedding she sent Glauce a beautiful white dress and a golden tiara.

Glauce was delighted with the gifts. She put them on, and admired herself in the mirror. Suddenly she screamed and collapsed, foaming at the mouth. A maid shouted for help, but by the time Jason and the king had arrived Glauce was engulfed in flames. Though she plunged into the fountain, the fire was not extinguished and when the king threw his arms round her, he was set alight, too.

The flames spread all through the palace, totally destroying it. Only Jason escaped by jumping from a window. Everyone else, including all the wedding guests, were burned to death. The angry citizens stormed Medea's house, but she had already fled. They then dragged out her children, and stoned them to death.

4. THE LAST LABOURS OF HERCULES

There are many conflicting reports of the Amazons who lived on the south coast of the Black Sea. Nobody knows exactly who they were...

THE QUEEN OF THE AMAZONS

When Hercules returned from his travels with the Argonauts, Eurystheus sent the hero back to the Black Sea to steal the golden belt of Ares from Hippolyta, queen of the Amazons.

The Amazons were a warlike race in which men and women had reversed their normal roles. The boys had their arms and legs broken at birth. Unable to fight or travel they did what was known as "women's work", whilst the girls were brought up as warriors.

Hercules and his men sailed through the Hellespont and up the Bosphorus where the Blue Rocks now stood fixed in place by Poseidon. When they reached their destination they found the Amazons assembled on the hillside.

"What brings you here?" asked Hippolyta. Hercules told her of the tasks he had to do for Eurystheus. The queen was attracted to the muscular hero, and agreed to give him the golden belt.

Hera watched them angrily from Mount Olympus. This was not the way she had planned it. The goddess disguised herself as an Amazon, joined the women on the hillside, and told them that Hercules intended to kidnap their queen. The Amazons jumped on their horses, and charged towards Hercules.

He suspected a carefully-planned ambush, and when Hippolyta refused to surrender the belt he knocked her to the ground. In the ensuing struggle he accidentally killed her with his club. Sad at heart, he removed the golden belt.

Though the Amazons fought on bravely, they were no match for Hercules and his men; Hercules soon called off the attack and carried the spoils back to Greece. He gave the golden belt to Eurystheus and dedicated Hippolyta's robes to Apollo at Delphi.

Hercules begged Hippolyta to surrender, but she tried to escape and in the scuffle he unintentionally killed her.

BEYOND THE END OF THE EARTH

Soon Eurystheus' herald was summoning Hercules again. The hero's last task was to bring back the cattle of Geryon.

Geryon was the grandson of Medusa and son of Chrysaor, the man with the golden sword who had risen from Medusa's neck when Perseus had killed her. He had the bodies of three men joined together, but with only one pair of legs, and was said to be the strongest man on earth. He lived on the isle of Erythia in the Atlantic Ocean.

Hercules set sail again. When he reached Erythia, he found the cattle were guarded by a giant herdsman with a two-headed dog. The dog bounded up to him, snarling, but Hercules crushed both its heads with a single blow from his club. A second blow despatched the herdsman.

Then suddenly Hercules saw Geryon, screaming abuse from his three mouths, and running down the hill with weapons in all six hands. Hercules threw himself to one side, and twisted round, shooting at Geryon over his shoulder.

Hera, who had been watching from Mount Olympus as usual, rushed to Geryon's aid. Hercules saw her out of the corner of his eye, and shot an arrow at her also. She screamed as it hit her, and vanished from sight.

Hercules transported the cattle back to the mainland, but his journey was far from over. He lost his way across the Alps and drove the cattle down through Italy. When he realised his mistake, he took them north again, but Hera sent a giant horsefly, which made the cattle stampede and scatter as far afield as the Black Sea.

Hercules was tired, but he laboriously rounded the cattle up again, and drove them down to Mycenae. His twelve years of labours were over at last. He hoped that he had seen the last of Eurystheus.

Hercules twisted round and shot an arrow that penetrated all three of Geryon's bodies in one shot.

55

THE GOLDEN APPLES

Eurystheus would not let Hercules live in peace, claiming that the killing of the Hydra was unacceptable.

"Why?" bellowed Hercules.

The herald trembled at the hero's angry tone. "Because you were helped by your nephew, Iolaus," he said. "In its place the king wants you to bring back the Golden Apples of the Hesperides from the Atlas Mountains."

"But they belong to Hera," said Hercules. "She will never let me have them."

The herald smiled, but said nothing.

Hercules had no choice but to return to the far end of the Mediterranean. The

Atlas was one of the Titans, and had built the wall around the Garden of the Hesperides. He had fought in the war between the giants and the gods, and as a punishment, Zeus had made him hold up the sky on his shoulders.

garden in which the apples grew was surrounded by a massive stone wall built by Atlas the Titan before he offended the gods and was sentenced to hold up the sky for ever. Round the apple tree was coiled the serpent, Ladon, who had a hundred heads, each of which spoke a different language.

As Hercules climbed the mountain above the garden, he saw Atlas, bowed double under the weight of the sky.

"I would do anything for a rest," groaned the Titan.

This gave Hercules an idea. He offered to hold up the sky if Atlas would steal the apples for him. He could see the serpent from where he stood, and, knowing that Atlas was afraid of it, Hercules shot it first with a poisoned arrow.

Atlas put the sky on Hercules' strong shoulders, and ran to pick the apples. He was back within a few minutes, carrying three of them, but instead of handing them to Hercules, he began to walk away.

"I will deliver them myself," he said.

Hercules thought fast, and called out to the Titan: "The sky is hurting my head. Would you hold it for a moment while I put a pad on it?"

Atlas lifted the sky off Hercules' shoulders. Thanking him, the hero picked up the apples and ran.

When he got back Eurystheus was too frightened to accept the apples, so Hercules gave them to Athena, who in turn returned them to Hera.

5. THE MINOTAUR

A PRINCE OF ATHENS

Aegeus, king of Athens, longed for a son. When he sought Medea's advice on the subject, she sent him to Troezen, to visit Pittheus the wise man. That night she cast a spell over the household, the wine flowed freely, and both Pittheus and Aegeus became very drunk. Pittheus then invited Aegeus to share his daughter Aethra's bed.

Next day Aegeus hid his dagger and sandals under a huge rock. "If you bear a son, wait till he is strong enough to move this rock," he told Aethra. "Then send him to me at Athens."

Aethra did bear a son, Theseus. One day, when he was a small boy, he attacked what he thought was an enormous lion with an axe. Suddenly, a huge man towered over him.

"That's only my lion's skin," he laughed. "I put it over a stool while I was eating."

The man was Hercules of Tiryns. Many years passed before Theseus met him again.

Young Theseus was inspired by the great hero, and longed to be like him. He grew up a strong and fearless young man. When he was sixteen, Aethra led him to the rock and told him to lift it, as Aegeus had instructed. He did so with ease, and found the dagger and sandals.

"Your father, the king of Athens, left them there for you," she explained. "And now you must go to him, taking the dagger and sandals with you."

Theseus wanted to prove himself a hero, so he travelled by the dangerous overland route. His adventures on the journey became known as the Labours of Theseus. He was waylaid by the evil

After many adventures Theseus finally reached Athens. Aegeus' palace was on the precipitous hill called the Acropolis. Athens hardly extended beyond this.

Sinis, who would tie his victims between two bent pine trees, then cut the trees loose, tearing his victims apart. Theseus overpowered Sinis, and gave him the same treatment.

Next Theseus was stopped by a huge bully called Sciron, who tried to kick him over a precipice; but Theseus caught him by the ankle and hurled him over instead.

There was another danger to come. Theseus met the inn-keeper Procrustes, who said he could offer a comfortable bed that would fit anyone. This was true, for if his victims were too short, Procrustes would stretch them, and if they were too tall, he would cut off their legs to fit. Theseus despatched him by cutting *him* down to size!

Finally, Theseus approached Athens.

Aegeus had left his sandals and dagger buried beneath a large rock. He told Aethra to send Theseus to Athens only when he could lift the rock.

MEDEA'S LAST CHANCE

When Theseus arrived at the citadel in Athens he made his way to the palace where a banquet was being held. He was unsure of his welcome, so he sat down quietly amongst the guests – but someone had noticed him.

Medea had fled to Athens for protection, and Aegeus had more than honoured his promise – he had married her. She bore him a son who would become king when Aegeus died. Instinctively she knew who the stranger was. She also knew that in order to inherit the throne Theseus must surely kill her son.

She told Aegeus that the young stranger in their midst had been sent by Pallas to assassinate him. Aegeus believed Medea, for Pallas and his sons had been trying to drive him from the throne for some years. He ordered a goblet of wine to be prepared, into which the sorceress emptied a phial of poison.

Then suddenly Aegeus noticed that the young man was cutting his meat with a dagger. He recognised it at once.

"You knew!" he shouted at Medea, knocking the goblet from her hand. "Get out of my sight. I never want to set eyes on you again!"

He then called Theseus to him, throwing his arms around his first-born son.

Medea harnessed her chariot, and fled with her son to Asia.

Medea poured a phial of poison into the drink Aegeus had prepared for Theseus.

The Minotaur, now fully grown, had developed a taste for human flesh.

THE MONSTROUS SON OF PASIPHAË

Theseus was eager to prove himself worthy of his father. He stopped a revolt led by Pallas, and hunted down the Cretan Bull, which was still terrorising the countryside. He brought it back alive, and sacrificed it to Apollo. But a greater test was to come. Some years earlier Aegeus had organised games, which were attended by athletes from all over the Greek world. The son of King Minos of Crete had won, but was killed by the other contestants. Minos held Aegeus responsible, and immediately declared war on Athens.

The gods took Minos' side, and sent down famine and disease on the city.

When Aegeus consulted the oracle at Delphi he was told that the city would only be spared if, every nine years, he sent a tribute of seven unmarried girls and seven youths to Crete, to be sacrificed to the Minotaur.

Minos had imprisoned Pasiphaë's grotesque half-human, half-bull son in a maze of passages beneath his palace, known as the labyrinth. Now fully grown, the Minotaur had developed a taste for human flesh.

His victims were chosen by lot, but before the first was drawn, Theseus had volunteered to go.

The ship they were to sail in had black sails, like a death ship. Before they left Athens, Theseus made a sacrifice to Aphrodite, goddess of love, imploring her to help them.

"May the gods bring you all back safely," said Aegeus, with tears in his eyes. He handed the captain a white sail. "If I see this white sail when the ship returns, I shall know you have been successful, and that the gods have spared us."

ARIADNE

When the ship reached Crete a ceremonial reception was prepared, attended by Minos and his family. As Theseus stepped ashore, Aphrodite intervened. She ordered Eros to shoot one of his love arrows into the heart of the king's daughter, Ariadne.

Ariadne did not have Medea's strength. She was completely overwhelmed by her love for Theseus. She desperately wanted to save him from the Minotaur, and she sought the help of the king's architect, Daedalus. Knowing that he had been an Athenian and one of Athens' greatest craftsmen, she hoped he might be prepared to help Theseus.

Daedalus had been held in great honour by Minos, for he had helped in the building of the magnificent palace at Knossos. But then the king discovered that it was Daedalus who had constructed the "cow machine" in which the queen, Pasiphaë, had pursued her unnatural love affair with the bull. The furious king then imprisoned Daedalus in the labyrinth with the Minotaur, but the queen helped him to escape.

Ariadne went to Daedalus in his secret hiding place, and the architect told her that Theseus' only hope was to kill the Minotaur before the sacrificial ceremony. Ariadne also learned how Theseus could find his way out of the labyrinth, once he had killed the monster.

King Minos arranged a reception for the fourteen victims, little suspecting that his daughter Ariadne would fall in love with Theseus.

THE MINOTAUR

A FIGHT TO THE DEATH

Theseus held on to the Minotaur's mane to stop the monster goring him, and stabbed it repeatedly.

That night Ariadne went to the building where the Athenians were being held. She promised to help Theseus, if he would take her away with him afterwards. When he agreed, she gave him a dagger, and a ball of thread.

"Use the thread to find your way out of the labyrinth," she said, as she led him through the gardens of the palace to the entrance. She tied the thread to the door-post, and told Theseus to unravel it as he went. It was pitch-black in the maze of passages, and many times Theseus had to retrace his steps, rewinding the ball of thread. Suddenly he heard loud snoring ahead of him and quickened his pace. Then he came to the room where the

Ariadne awoke to see Theseus sailing away. Was it a mistake, or had the Athenian hero deliberately deserted her?

Minotaur lay sleeping. He could just see its bull-like head with horns, and its long mane hanging over its forehead.

As Theseus crept forward the Minotaur woke and hurled a rock at him. Theseus ducked, then dashed in, grabbing its mane, so that the beast could not gore him. He grasped a horn, but it broke off. Then he plunged his dagger into the Minotaur's neck. It roared in pain and tried to crush him, but Theseus stabbed again and again, until its grip weakened. The Minotaur was dead!

Theseus made his way back, winding up the ball of thread as he went. As he emerged into the moonlight Ariadne was waiting for him.

"Quick," urged Theseus. "We must release the others and return to the ship."

When Theseus and his companions reached the beach, they holed the Cretan ships, and then spent the night on an offshore island. Athena woke them at dawn.

"You must leave quickly, for Minos knows what has happened," she said.

Soon they were rowing far out to sea, not relaxing until they were sure Minos would not catch them. But in their haste, they left Ariadne behind. She watched weeping as the ship's black sail disappeared over the horizon. Some say she hanged herself in despair, but others claim that the wine god Bacchus found her and married her.

A SAD HOMECOMING

As Theseus' ship rounded the headland into the Bay of Phaleron, he could see with a terrible sense of foreboding that his father was not there to welcome them.

"We thought you were dead!" cried the citizens.

Theseus was grief-stricken. He had forgotten to change the sail. His father had thrown himself from the cliffs when he saw the black-sailed ship, believing his son had been killed by the Minotaur.

DAEDALUS' FLIGHT

When Minos learned that Daedalus had helped Ariadne and the Athenians, he was determined to kill the architect.

Daedalus knew that he and his son, Icarus, must escape from Crete. He made two pairs of wings from birds' feathers, sticking them together with wax. Then he strapped them to their shoulders, and they both flew off over the sea. Icarus loved the feeling that he could fly, and soared towards the sun. But the sun's heat melted the wax and the boy plunged to his death. Sadly Daedalus flew on to Sicily alone, where King Cocalus gave him shelter.

Minos had a plan to catch Daedalus. He searched the Mediterranean; reaching Sicily, he produced a spiral seashell, and asked if anyone could thread it. Cocalus took the shell to Daedalus, who drilled a hole in the top of the shell, and fixed a thread to an ant, who followed the spiral till it came out of the hole at the top. Minos knew then that he had found Daedalus. But Daedalus was popular with the king's daughters, because he made them such wonderful toys, and Cocalus was not prepared to hand him over. One night they made Minos drunk, and killed him in his bath.

Daedalus made two pairs of wings with which he and his son Icarus made their escape from Knossos. The vast palace at Knossos made the palaces of mainland Greece seem very small and insignificant.

THE DEATH OF AN AMAZON QUEEN

Theseus, now king of Athens, was restless. He longed for the heroic life again, and so he led an expedition to the land of the Amazons where he abducted their new queen, Antiope, bringing her back to Athens as his concubine.

The Amazons joined the Scythians in an invasion of Greece in order to rescue their queen, but by now Antiope had fallen in love with Theseus, and persuaded them to withdraw.

Although Antiope bore Theseus a son, it was the beautiful Phaedra he truly loved and planned to marry. On the day of the wedding, Antiope burst in on the feast, fully armed, but was killed in the ensuing fight. Theseus then asked his grandfather, Pittheus, to adopt Antiope's son, Hippolytus.

Phaedra bore Theseus several sons, and it seemed that nothing could spoil their happiness. But the gods had other plans. Theseus met Pirithous, king of the Lapiths, a barbarous tribe from the mountains of Thessaly. The two became great friends, and Theseus was invited to Pirithous' wedding. It was there that he came across Hercules again. Several centaurs had also been invited; though Pirithous tried to keep them from the wine, they became drunk, and dragged Pirithous' bride away by her hair and killed her.

A long war between Lapiths and centaurs followed, in which Hercules and Theseus were both involved. The centaurs were finally defeated, and driven from Thessaly.

THE TRAGEDY OF PHAEDRA

Meanwhile, back in Athens, something was afoot that would wreck Theseus' life and ultimately cause his death.

Theseus' son, Hippolytus, had offended Aphrodite, and the goddess took her revenge by making his stepmother, Phaedra, fall in love with him. Phaedra could neither eat nor sleep for thinking of Hippolytus, and at last she told him of her passion. Hippolytus was horrified, and wanted nothing to do with her. Then Phaedra's love turned to hate. She accused Hippolytus of assaulting her, then took her own life.

When Theseus returned, he believed the dreadful story and asked the gods for vengeance. Hippolytus fled from Athens, taking the precipitous Corinth road Theseus had followed years before. As he drove along, Poseidon sent an enormous wave thundering towards the cliff, with a sea monster riding on its crest. Hippolytus' horses dashed wildly in panic; the reins caught on an olive tree, and he was dragged over the cliffs to his death.

Phaedra watched secretly as Hippolytus trained for the games. Her unnatural passion for her stepson was to end in tragedy for them both.

THE HOUND OF HELL

The death of his wife affected Theseus' mind. He sought out his friend Pirithous and together they abducted the beautiful Helen of Troy. They drew lots for her, agreeing that the winner should help the loser abduct another woman. Theseus won, and left Helen in his mother's care while he and Pirithous asked the oracle who this other woman should be.

The priestess thought they were drunk. She mockingly suggested Persephone, wife of Hades, god of the Underworld. "We cannot do that!" protested Theseus, but Pirithous was determined that he should keep his word. They descended into the Underworld and Hades met them at the gates. He demanded to know what they wanted.

Above: *Charon ferried Hercules across the river Styx to the gates of Hell. It was customary to bury money with a corpse to pay the ferryman, but Charon was so terrified of Hercules that he ferried him across for nothing.*

Left: *Cerberus, watchdog of the Underworld, was generally believed to have three heads, a snake's tail and innumerable snakes' heads along its back.*

"We have come for your wife, Persephone," said Theseus.

"Sit down, and I will think about it," said Hades calmly, but when they did so, the god sealed them to their seats so they could not move. And there they stayed, tormented by the Furies and savaged by the watchdog, Cerberus.

Meanwhile Hercules was again summoned by Eurystheus, who insisted that the cleaning of the Augeian stables was not a true labour, since Augeias had given him some cattle for doing it.

"You must capture Cerberus, Hades' watchdog," said Eurystheus.

It was impossible, but once again Athena came to his aid. The goddess revived his flagging spirits, and the hero descended to the river Styx. Hercules so terrified the ferryman that he was immediately rowed across to the land of the dead. By now Theseus and Pirithous had been in hell for four long years.

Persephone agreed to let both men go, if Hercules himself released them. The strong man managed to rescue Theseus, but they had to leave Pirithous behind, for he could not break Hades' seal.

Now Hercules had to catch Cerberus. Hades gave him permission to do this, provided the hero caught the beast with his bare hands.

"He's a good dog," said Hades. "I won't allow you to use your club or poison against him."

The three-headed dog snarled as Hercules approached, but he seized it by the throat. It tried to shake him off but Hercules hung on grimly, until the dog finally rolled on its back in surrender. Hercules trussed it with its own chain, and brought it into the world of the living.

71

THE HYDRA'S REVENGE

Theseus returned home to find that Helen's brothers had conquered Athens, placing a new king on the throne, and making Theseus' mother a slave.

Theseus retired to the island of Skyros, broken-hearted. One day he was walking on the cliff, when he was either pushed or fell to his death.

Jason, too, died about this time. The Argonaut had left Corinth after the death of Glauce and his children, and had wandered aimlessly for years. Now old and penniless, he returned to Corinth to take a last look at the *Argo*. He sat down by the side of the ship's crumbling hulk, remembering his past days of glory. Suddenly there was a loud crack, the rotten timbers broke and the figurehead crashed on him, killing him where he sat.

Hercules was still plagued by his violent temper, and he killed friends and enemies alike. He sought advice from the Pythoness at Delphi, but when she refused to help him, he wrecked the shrine in a fit of rage. As a punishment he was sold into slavery. When he was released after three years, he crossed the Corinthian gulf and settled in Calydon, but his troubles followed him and he was forced to move on.

Accompanied by his second wife, Deianira, Hercules reached the river Evenus where the centaur, Nessus, operated the ferry. First Nessus took Hercules across the river, then returned for Deianira. Thinking Hercules could not see him, the centaur tried to assault Deianira, but Hercules heard her screams, and shot Nessus.

"Save some of my blood," the dying centaur gasped to Deianira. "It will act as a love charm."

Hercules and Deianira were given sanctuary in Trachis, but the hero's violent nature continued to govern him.

He sacked Oechalia, killing the king, and dragging his daughter Iole off as his concubine.

Returning by sea, he stopped at the Cenaeum promontory across the bay from Trachis, to offer sacrifice to his father, Zeus. He sent a messenger to collect his best tunic, and began to build an altar.

Deianira heard from the messenger about what had happened at Oechalia, and that Iole was now with Hercules. With tears in her eyes, she fetched her husband's best red tunic, and, remembering the centaur's words, sprinkled its blood on the garment.

When Hercules put on the tunic, the heat from his body activated the Hydra's venom in the centaur's blood. It ate into his skin like acid. He ripped off the tunic, but his flesh tore away with it. He knew there was no cure. He asked to be carried to Mount Oeta, where a funeral pyre was built and Hercules laid upon it. Writhing in agony, he begged his companions to light the pyre but they refused. Finally a passing shepherd set it alight and Hercules died at last, the greatest of all the Greek heroes.

"Save some of my blood," the dying centaur begged. "It will act as a love charm."

72

6. FACT OR FICTION?

Above: Plan of Tiryns showing the palace (yellow), the early walls (red) and the late walls (black).

Above: The citadel of Tiryns, the most strongly fortified of the Mycenaean citadels, as it might have appeared in 1250 BC.

Above: Section through the galleries in the south wall of the citadel of Tiryns.

A LOST CIVILISATION

Until about 125 years ago, scholars believed that the Greek legends were just fairy tales. But everything changed when the archaeologist, Heinrich Schliemann, discovered the remains of ancient Troy, Mycenae and Tiryns. It is now known that the places connected with the great legends were centres of a civilisation that flourished a thousand years before the Greek classical period. Bronze Age citadels and palaces have been discovered at Thebes, Orchomenos, Athens, Iolcos, Tiryns and Mycenae, which has given its name, Mycenaean, to this civilisation.

Tiryns, the most impressive of the Mycenaean citadels, is built on a low rock rising some 18 metres above the surrounding plain. The remains that one sees today, reconstructed above, date from the end of the Bronze Age in the thirteenth century BC. The fortified palace had been built on the highest point of the rock about 1500 BC (see above, in yellow). This may be associated with Perseus. It was a typical Mycenaean palace centred on a megaron, a large hall or throne room, with a roof, supported by four columns (see right). Fortifications were added to the north and south of the building about 1425 BC (in red). Finally, around 1300 BC, the south and east walls were reinforced with galleries, chambers in the walls from which archers could beat off besiegers, and the town at the north end was included in the circuit (above).

74

Right: Cutaway section of the palace showing the entrance, vestibule and throne room.

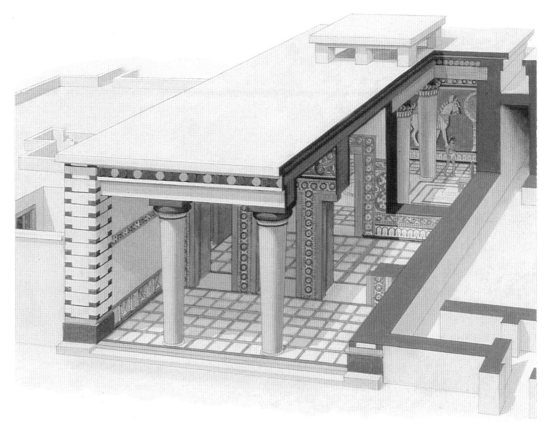

Below: The megaron of the palace at Tiryns. Enough of the floor remained to reconstruct the decoration. The rest is based on other Mycenaean palaces.

THE PALACE OF MINOS

Cutaway section of the domestic quarter of the great palace at Knossos, Crete. This is only about one sixth of the whole vast palace complex. The grand stairway (2) was built into the side of the hill. The remains of the ground and first floors have survived. There was at least one more floor above it.
1. Central courtyard.
2. Grand staircase.
3. Hall of the Double Axes. This was the throne room.
4. Queen's room.
5. Queen's bathroom.

Below: Plan of the whole palace. The domestic quarter is marked in red.
1. The central courtyard.
2. The west court.

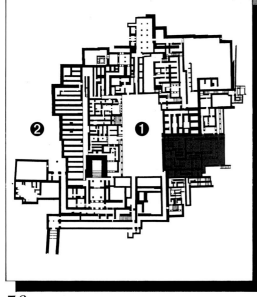

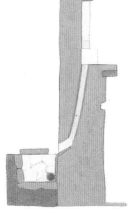

Left: Section of the wall of the West House showing the pipe leading from the first floor toilet to the sewage chamber. The sewage ran through a pipe to the main sewer under the street.

Above: An exploded cutaway section of the West House at Thera showing the lower and upper floors. The living quarters were on the upper floor. Two of these rooms were highly decorated. A = Toilet.

Above: Part of the excavations at Thera showing houses with pots outside just as they were when the volcano erupted 3,500 years ago.

Above: One of the tiny models of houses discovered at Knossos. They show timber-framed stone buildings.

Right: The sewer running beneath the main street in Thera.

LIFE IN A BRONZE AGE TOWN

About 1500 BC the volcano on the island of Thera in the Aegean Sea erupted, burying towns and villages on the island, and causing devastation as far away as Crete.

Excavations begun in 1967 have started to uncover a complete town at Akroteri at the southern end of the island. Houses up to four storeys high have been found lining cobbled streets. Sewers run through clay pipes beneath the streets. The houses are built of uncut stones, reinforced with wooden joists, with square-cut masonry at the corners.

The ground floors were often used as workshops and store rooms. The living rooms were upstairs, and were connected by staircases. Many of the rooms are decorated with wall paintings which tell us much about the people who lived there.

THE SHIPS OF THERA

Right: Part of the fresco from the West House at Thera. The larger ships which are probably taking part in a religious festival are being paddled as canoes. The smaller ship is being rowed as a galley. The ships are steered in the ancient fashion by large steering oars at the stern.

Below: A 'rearcastle' of a ship. It is covered with cow hides. This is one of a series of such cabins illustrated in one of the upstairs rooms of the West House at Thera.

Archaeologists excavating the upstairs rooms of the West House at Thera found fragments of a wall painting showing a procession of ships, which has increased our knowledge of the ships of this period.

But the painting also raises a number of problems. The ships in the painting are being paddled like canoes, an inefficient method that was already obsolete by this time. Yet the Therans clearly knew about the more modern and efficient method of rowing, since one of the smaller boats is indeed being rowed. The confusion is increased by what appears to be a ram at the rear end instead of the front of the ship.

It has been suggested that the painting shows a religious festival, and that the ships are being paddled to conform to a religious practice. If the ship is going backwards, then the steersman with his large oar has changed ends.

Above: Three Bronze Age stone anchors from the eastern Mediterranean. The two wooden stakes which were fitted through holes in the top stone are restored.

If the ship could be reversed for battle, a Y-shaped projection on the prow of the main ship in the illustration might be for the steering oar. This is supported by the fact that the earliest Greek warships, c.800–500 BC, all have forecastles. Most scholars, however, disagree with this theory. They argue that the protrusion at the back of the ship is not a ram and that the ship is going forwards, though no satisfactory alternative for the 'ram' has yet been suggested.

The Theran ships also have sails like most other ancient oared ships. The mast of the ship in the picture has combs on either side at the top for raising the sail. The furled sail rests on top of the canopy which covers the passengers, and is held in place by forked supports similar to those on Viking ships.

Above: A reconstruction of one of the ships from Thera as a galley with the lion figurehead and 'ram' at the front. This is controversial. Most scholars think that the far end is in fact the front of the ship.

81

GODS AND MEN

Although Zeus and Poseidon were the most powerful of the Greek gods, it was the goddesses, Athena, Hera and Aphrodite, who helped or opposed the heroes.

It has become increasingly evident as more sites are excavated that Bronze Age peoples mainly worshipped female gods. All the idols from Crete are female, the two most famous being the snake goddesses from Knossos. There can be little doubt that the Cretans' supreme deity was also a goddess. They may have worshipped only one goddess and maybe her son, brother or husband, who died each autumn to be born again the following spring. This belief was common in the Middle East, reflecting the cycle of the seasons.

The Mycenaeans seem to have had their own gods which included Zeus, Poseidon, Hera, Hermes and Athena. These are mentioned on late Mycenaean writing tablets. They were probably brought to Greece by the Greek-speaking peoples who invaded the country and settled there about 1900 BC. They also adopted the Cretan goddess whom they worshipped as Artemis, goddess of wild animals. She was the supreme deity of the Mycenaeans.

At the end of the thirteenth century BC the Mycenaean civilisation rapidly declined and Greece plunged into a dark age. This affected the whole of the Middle East. The Hittite empire collapsed and there were massive migrations from the north.

The end of the Bronze Age civilisations may have been caused by a climatic change. This would account for a religious change that also took place in Greece, and in other parts of the eastern Mediterranean. The mother goddess lost her supreme position to the weather god. When Greece emerged from the dark age in the eighth century BC, Zeus the thunderer had become king of the gods and Artemis had dropped to a lower status.

Above: A statue of a snake goddess found in the palace at Knossos in Crete. Made about 1650 BC, it probably represents the main deity of Crete, the mother goddess. The statuette on page 85 may show the same goddess.

82

Right: Gold ring from Tiryns showing a goddess sitting on a folding chair with a bird behind her. She is being approached by four daemons, minor supernatural beings, carrying offerings.

Right: A painting of a priestess from the West House at Thera. Priestesses are a very common feature of Cretan and Mycenaean religion.

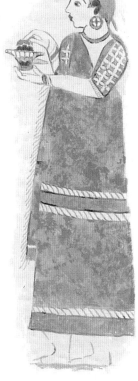

Above: A fragment of a wall painting from the palace at Tiryns showing a daemon very similar to those on the gold ring at the top of the page.

Left: An offering table decorated with dolphins from the West House at Thera. It was used for burning offerings to the gods.

Left: Horns of consecration from Knossos in Crete. These were used to decorate religious buildings.

Left: An ornamental gold plaque found at Mycenae, showing a small temple or shrine c.1550 BC. The Mycenaeans did not build large temples like the later Greeks.

Right: A priestess preparing to offer sacrifice in front of a shrine. This is part of a painted sarcophagus from Hagia Triada in Crete.

COSTUME

The wall paintings and other representations from both Crete and mainland Greece show that before about 1300 BC men generally wore only a loincloth. Some Mycenaean examples show men in a more elaborate kilt, flounced in a similar fashion to women's dress. Men are also sometimes shown wearing boots.

Women wore more elaborate dress but are always shown barefoot. Their clothes consisted of a full-length dress open down the front to below the waist, leaving the breasts bare. A flounced skirt or kilt was worn over this.

Both men and women wore jewellery. Women painted their finger and toe nails, and no doubt used facial make-up. Both men and women usually had very long hair, although young boys and girls often had their heads partially shaved, possibly for religious purposes.

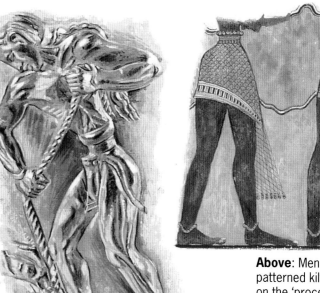

Above: Men wearing patterned kilts shown on the 'procession' fresco from the palace at Knossos in Crete, c.1475 BC.

Above: A man dressed in the traditional Cretan loincloth and laced-up boots, from a gold cup discovered at Vapheio in southern Greece, c.1500 BC.

Left: A man dressed in a full-length garment, playing a lyre. This painting on a sarcophagus from Hagia Triada in Crete is one of the few illustrations of men in full-length clothes.

Right: A hero in a flounced kilt fighting a lion, from an early Mycenaean seal. These kilts would appear to be identical to those worn by women (see opposite page).

Left: The partially shaven head of a boy from the 'boxers' fresco discovered in the House of the Antelopes in Thera.

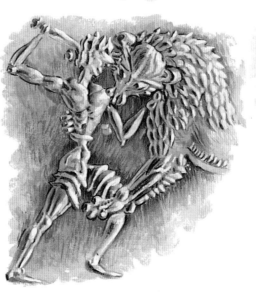

Above: The partially shaven head of a youth from the West House at Thera.

Right: The upper part of a woman, from a fresco at Knossos. She wears a bodice open at the front to leave her breasts uncovered.

Left: The famous 'La Parisienne' fresco from the palace at Knossos. The girl wears a sacral knot at the back of her neck, identifying her as a priestess.

Above: A snake goddess from Knossos c.1650 BC, wearing a full-length dress with flounced skirt covered by a kind of apron. The dress looks very similar to fashions early this century.

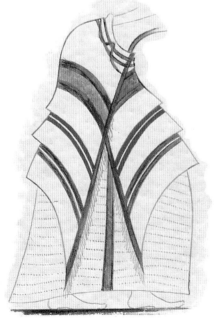

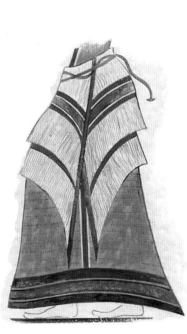

Left: Dresses with kilts shown on paintings from Thera.

Above: A gold earring in the form of two wasps found at Mallia in Crete, c.2000 BC.

The frescos from Thera (see overleaf) show women wearing fine jewellery.

85

THE WOMEN OF THERA

The illustrations on this page all come from one room in a house at Thera. They show the beauty and variety of women's dress about 1500 BC. There are young girls with their heads partially shaved, mature women with a full head of hair arranged in a variety of styles, and older women with their hair covered. All wear jewellery but only younger women have earrings.

86

HEROES AND MONSTERS

THE HYDRA

Most legends are corrupted and embellished accounts of real events. They are often further confused because several different stories have been condensed into one. There are also many variations of the same story. A good example of this is the Hydra, which was said to have 8, 9, 50, 100 or 10,000 heads.

There is almost certainly a real event underlying the Hydra story (page 22). The word 'hydra' means water. We know that the Mycenaeans drained marshes. Their drainage works have been found around Lake Copais in central Greece. Such swamps would be infested with water snakes and a source of many infectious diseases. As the engineers tried to block off one source of water, two or three more would burst out. The main water supply could not be dammed but had to be channelled away. Here are all the elements of the Hydra story.

THE GOLDEN FLEECE

The least disguised of these historical events is the quest for the Golden Fleece (page 30). This records attempts by Mycenaean seamen to open up trade with the peoples of the Black Sea. Even as late as the middle of this century, miners in Russian Georgia (ancient Colchis) collected gold dust by staking out sheepskins in mountain streams.

Some of Hercules' later labours probably record the opening of trade links with Spain, the western end of north Africa and the fabulous islands beyond the Pillars of Hercules (Straits of Gibraltar).

A UNIVERSAL HERO

Hercules is a patchwork figure coming from all places and all times. He is basically a Stone Age hunter hero. Almost identical figures can be found in many other cultures. The Babylonian hero, Gilgamesh, kills a lion and wears its skin. He also performs another of Hercules' labours, the golden apples (page

Above: The people of Colchis used to place sheepskins in mountain streams to collect gold dust.

Left: One of the many sculptures of bulls found in Crete. This example was found at Knossos.

Right: A double axe from the sanctuary in the Arkalochori cave in Crete. The double axe was a sacred symbol often found in shrines.

56). There is a Phoenician figurine which is identical to Hercules; and of course Samson in the Bible kills a lion bare-handed.

MINOS AND DAEDALUS

The story of Minos' pursuit of Daedalus to Sicily and his death on the island (page 66) probably records a real historical event. There is archaeological evidence of a strong Cretan influence in Sicily and the heel of Italy in the fourteenth century BC. It is possible that Minos tried to overrun Sicily but was defeated and killed. His army may have escaped to the heel of Italy and settled there.

THE GODDESS OF LOVE

The Perseus and Andromeda story (page 14) recalls the introduction of the Phoenician love goddess, Ishtar-Astarte, into Greece. Later Greeks admitted that Aphrodite, their goddess of love, came from Phoenicia.

MONSTERS, REAL AND MYTHICAL

Lions and bulls which play an important role in the legends also figure very prominently in Mycenaean art. This is not surprising, as the lion was the most dangerous and the bull the strongest animal the Mycenaeans knew. A dagger from Mycenae shows a lion hunt, and a beautiful gold cup from Vapheio in Greece shows a bull hunt.

Some of the mythical beasts the heroes fought might not be as fantastic as they seem. The centaur, half man and half horse (page 24), is not a figment of Greek imagination. Centaurs came from Thessaly which, unlike mountainous southern Greece, was suited to horsemen. Never having seen men riding horses, the prehistoric Greeks made the same mistake as the Incas of South America nearly 3000 years later when they saw Spanish cavalry. They assumed that man and horse were one creature.

THESEUS IN GREECE

Theseus' Cretan adventure has fascinated people for 3000 years. It is generally accepted that the Cretan navy controlled the Aegean. Athens and other coastal towns were probably forced to send hostages to the hated King Minos. This seems reasonable; but what about the Labyrinth and what about the Minotaur?

Above: A decorated dagger blade from Mycenae showing a lion hunt. The lion is very accurately drawn – the artist must have seen a real lion.

Below: Part of the decoration of the Vapheio gold cup, showing a bull hunt. One bull has been caught in a rope net but another has escaped and gored two of the hunters.

Left: A fresco from the palace at Knossos showing two girls and a boy in the various stages of bull jumping.

Below: Bull jumping in the courtyard of the palace at Knossos. Some circus acrobats and bull fighters claim this feat is impossible. It was certainly exceedingly dangerous.

THE BULL JUMPERS

Anyone visiting the site of Knossos and the Museum at Heraklion where most of the small finds are kept cannot help noticing that two objects recur again and again: representations of bulls and double axes. The Greek for a double axe is 'labrys'. Double axe symbols are carved all over the walls of the large throne room at Knossos, and no doubt it was called the Hall of the Double Axes, or "Labyrinth". Mainland Greeks at the time were accustomed to simple palaces. The great complexity of Knossos would have caused people to get lost and so the legend of the labyrinth arose.

Many paintings and sculptures from Crete show youths and young girls performing incredibly dangerous acrobatic feats. A bull charges with its head lowered, an acrobat grips its horns and uses the bull's tossing action to perform a somersault in mid air and land on the bull's back. Many youngsters must have been killed doing this. The discovery of children's bones at Knossos with knife marks on them implies child sacrifice. Add a little imagination and one has the Minotaur legend.

Left: A diagram showing the four stages of bull jumping.

Right: Part of the decoration of a black steatite jug showing an acrobat misjudging his jump and landing on the bull's horns.

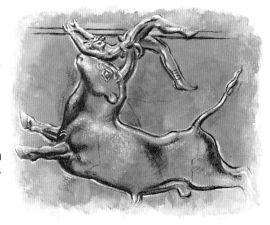

INDEX

First published in 1993 by Simon & Schuster Young Books.   Reprinted 1994 by Macdonald Young Books
Campus 400 Maylands Avenue Hemel Hempstead Herts HP2 7EZ   © Peter Connolly 1993
ISBN 0 7500 1016 9   All rights reserved   Printed and bound in Hong Kong by Wing King Tong